HOW TO X YOUR EX

A GUIDE TO GETTING PAST UNHEALTHY RELATIONSHIPS

WORKBOOK

ISBN: 979-8-5617970-8-8

Cover and interior typesetting by Gaia Design Studio

Second Edition

CONTENTS

CONTENTS   3

INTRO   5

CURRENT BREAKUP   7

JOURNALING   9

PHASE 1: LET IT OUT   11

PHASE 2: THIS IS NOT A CONTACT SPORT,
CUT IT OUT   21

PHASE 3: REBOUNDS ARE ONLY GOOD IN
BASKETBALL   27

PHASE 4: THE CLOSURE TRAP   31

PHASE 5: GIVE IT TO YOUR GOD   35

PHASE 6: PERCEPTION IS REALITY   43

PHASE 7: FIGHTING LONELY   55

PHASE 8: SELF-REFLECTION   63

PHASE 9: SIT IN IT   69

PHASE 10: RECLAIM YOUR THOUGHTS   77

CONCLUSION   83

APPENDIX   87

INTRO

How do you normally get over breakups?

....

....

....

....

....

....

Have you found your current strategy to be helpful or harmful?

....

....

....

....

....

Pros to current strategy:

- ✓   *I feel less upset*
- ✓   *I don't miss them as much*
- ✓ ....
- ✓ ....
- ✓ ....
- ✓ ....

Cons to current strategy:

- ✓   *I find myself stalking their social media*
- ✓   *I never seem to be completely over my exes*
- ✓ ....
- ✓ ....
- ✓ ....
- ✓ ....

If your current strategy's pros outweigh the cons, then maybe you can continue to use it. But if you find that the cons outweigh the pros, it's time to eliminate your current way of getting over your ex and adopt a new way.

CURRENT BREAKUP

What led to your breakup?

....

....

....

....

....

Were you genuinely happy in the relationship? **Yes or No**

....

....

....

Is there anything you could've done to change the outcome of the relationship? (*Settling for something you do not want is not an answer.*)

....

....

....

....

....

....

....

....

....

....

....

....

....

JOURNALING

Journaling is a great tool for healing. You have the ability to be totally vulnerable and genuine because only you get to see your journal entries. It's also a form of release. Too often, we internalize our true feelings of brokenness because we think it makes us look weak. That's not healthy and it can prolong the healing process. That is why after every phase, you'll be asked to enter a journal entry in the Appendix. Flip to page 83 to write your first journal entry.

PHASE 1
LET IT OUT

The first phase is all about letting it out. In order to start emotionally heal, one must first unload how they really feel. One of the best tools is *Letter to Your Ex*. Below is my letter to my ex. Reread it if you need a point of reference.

LETTER TO YOUR EX EXAMPLE...

Dear ...., (Put your ex's name here? Try it.)

It kills me how men can come into your life, fuck it up, then vanish, leaving you to figure out where it all went wrong. How dare you?! Here I was minding my own business, living my sweet life and here you come asking me for a second chance. If you weren't ready to give your all then why interrupt the greatness I had going on? What's crazy is, I don't even give second chances but I gave you one because I thought you deserved it. HA! The only thing you deserve is to be slapped upside that weird shaped head of yours. I can still remember our lunch date when you delivered a bunch of sugar coated lies like "This is our year" and "I would never hurt you". Well guess what; YOU HURT ME!

When I came to visit you in North Dakota, everything was awesome. I met your married friends and they were even trying to convince me to move there. I thought we reached another level of our relationship but that was a huge misconception. When I got home, we barely talked. I would text you back to back and wouldn't get a reply

for hours. You ignored every single FaceTime call just to say you were busy working extra shifts. I told myself to let it go because I knew you would be in Atlanta in a few weeks. When you came here, you treated me like a second-hand groupie. Out of three days, I saw you a total of ve hours. How the hell are you going to tell me you're coming to Atlanta to see me and only give me ve freaking hours of your time?

Oh and let's not forget the hotel incident. I booked us one of the nicest hotels in the city for a romantic evening. I waited hours for you just to get a text saying you can't make it right before midnight. Wow...I can't believe you did that to me and I still came to church with you and your mother on that Sunday hoping it could salvage the remnants of our relationship. Why would you introduce me to your mom knowing you were about to leave me? There is a special place in hell for men like you.

It hurts so much because I let my guard down. I went against my "no second chances" rule and I let you in. I had no defense up with you and you took advantage of that. What I can't understand is why a huge part of me blames myself for part of this. I knew you were a 'playa' in your past so why would I believe you? I knew what you were capable of but I told myself I had to let go of that past in order to give us a try. See men always complain that women can't let go of the past but that's a lie. I let go for you! But how do you repay me? You throw me away like last week's leftovers. See this is the type of bull that makes those bitter black women everyone likes to talk about. Men come into our lives with horrible intentions and when they break our hearts we have to put the pieces back together. No wonder why so many black women have bitchy attitudes and emotional walls as big as the Wall of China. But I won't give you that power. I will NOT allow you to steal joy from me any longer. You had your chance and I know that karma is a pretty little bitch and she will come back around. As for me, the best revenge is living well and that is exactly what I am going to do. So damn you and that cold ass North Dakota because this is goodbye!

Now it's your turn. Write your letter to your ex. Remember, this is for your eyes only. They'll never see this.

LETTER TO YOUR EX

ARE YOU READY FOR A FACE TO FACE DIALOGUE?

After a breakup, we can't wait to tell our ex how we feel. We think we're ready to speak to them face to face so we can "get it off our chest". As mentioned in the book, we're rarely ready for this kind of dialogue. Here's a checklist that outlines what it looks like when you're actually ready for a face to face conversation.

CHECK ALL THAT APPLY, BE HONEST

- [ ] *You can discuss your ex with others without crying or getting upset*
- [ ] *You are sleeping well after the breakup*
- [ ] *You are NOT drinking, using drugs, and/or partying to distract you from the emotions you feel for your ex.*
- [ ] *You do NOT feel a strong urge to physically harm your ex.*

☐   *You do NOT want them back.*

☐   *You do NOT desire an apology because you can move on without it.*

If you can answer yes to all of these, then you are ready for a face to face meeting with your ex. DO NOT lie to yourself and say yes when you know you're not ready. It'll only set you back in your healing process.

FACE TO FACE SCRIPT

If you are truly ready to see your ex, make sure you know exactly what you're going to say. Always write down your points beforehand so you don't get side tracked. In highly emotional circumstances, it's easy to let your emotions talk and your logic take a backseat. Nope, that is why you're going in with your notes. You only need to express 3 things...

1. *You hurt me*

2. *Here's why*

3. *I'm moving on because*

That's it, that's all. This is not a meeting to rekindle anything, you are just letting it out. This meeting is honestly not necessary but I know some people want to release their emotions so that is what you're doing. You can listen to them but again, the goal is to have an emotional release so you can move on. If your intention is to do anything other than that, do NOT meet up with them.

▶ ***Turn to the Appendix for your next journal entry.***

PHASE 2
THIS IS NOT A CONTACT SPORT, CUT IT OUT

Are you still in contact with your ex? Yes or No

....

Contact includes you reaching out to them and them having

access to reach out to you.

If yes, why?

....

....

…………………………………………………………………………

…………………………………………………………………………

…………………………………………24…………………………………

*What percentage of commitment to you have in x'ing
your ex?*

…………………………………………………………………………

…………………………………………………………………………

…………………………………………………………………………

Moving on from an ex isn't easy. The great part is you don't have to do it alone. Make a list of accountability partners you can call when you are tempted to contact your ex or when you begin to regret your decision. These should be individuals who are in support of your happiness and your growth and who will be honest with you. Contact them and explain to them what you are doing and why you need them to hold you accountable.

ACCOUNTABILITY PARTNERS

Name: ....

They will hold me accountable for ....

....

Name: ....

They will hold me accountable for ....

....

Name: ....

They will hold me accountable for ....

....

Name: ....

They will hold me accountable for ....

....

Name: ....

They will hold me accountable for ....

....

Name: ....

They will hold me accountable for ....

....

REFOCUSING...

One of the hardest parts of moving on is the discomfort that comes from not speaking to someone that you're accustomed to speaking to everyday. This is why you need to re-direct your energy towards something more productive. What is something you've been needing to complete? What's a hobby you've been wanting to try but haven't gotten around to? What friends or family have you been neglecting that you can now hang out and catch up with? What about your health and fitness goals?

Make a list of things you can re-focus your energy on during this time of healing.

- ....
- ....
- ....
- ....
- ....
- ....
- ....
- ....
- ....
- ....
- ....
- ....

ASHLEIGH'S QUICK TIP

Remember to keep your 'Letter to Your Ex' close so you can reread it to remind you of why you ended the relationship. Keep your eye on the prize which is healing and wholeness.

▶ **Turn to the Appendix for your next journal entry.**

PHASE 3
REBOUNDS ARE ONLY GOOD IN BASKETBALL

Have you ever dated someone to get over an ex?

Let me rephrase...

Have you ever dated someone before you were fully healed emotionally from an ex? It's okay to be honest, I'm sure 95% of people have.

Think about your most recent encounter with a *rebound*.

When did you feel the urge to start dating them? Imme-diately after the breakup or once the reality of the breakup kicked in?

....

....

....

- *Did you find yourself comparing them to your ex? .....*

  ....

- *When they disappointed you, did you find yourself thinking of your ex more? ....*

  ....

- *In the end, can you actually say the rebound helped you to eliminate the feelings you have for your ex? .....*

  ....

I hope you're being honest with yourself because the answer should easily be no.

Rebounds distract, they don't eliminate any emotions from your previous relationship. Once the rebound is done, you'll still be left to deal with the hurt from your breakup.

REMEMBER THE REBOUND CHARACTERISTICS…

- [ ] *They are not your typical type*
- [ ] *You move really fast*
- [ ] *You had sex immediately and it was good*
- [ ] *You have no direction for the relationship*
- [ ] *You randomly talk about your ex*
- [ ] *You entertain everyone*

If 3 or more are true, then it's a rebound.

In the last phase, you were advised to write a list of things to re-focus your energy on. That's the best way to combat rebounds. You need to fill your time with healthy distractions and dating without emotionally healing from an ex is not healthy.

▶ ***Turn to the Appendix for your next journal entry.***

PHASE 4
THE CLOSURE TRAP

*Do you **need** closure?*

....

....

....

Why or why not?

....

....

....

Most times, we aren't attached to the person. We are attached to what they provided for us. On page 49, I spoke about how Orlando provided self-love at a time when I didn't feel it for myself. I was attached to the feeling he gave me when all the while I was supposed to be giving myself that; with or without him.

Think deeply about what your ex may have provided. What emotion are you attached to? It could be security because they provided for you. It could be peace because they always helped you through tough days. It could simply be love because maybe you never actually felt it anywhere else. Take a moment and write out what it could be.

....

....

....

....

....

....

....

....

....

....

....

Although it may be uncomfortable, we can provide for ourselves most emotions any other person provides for us. For me, I had to spend some time by myself to figure out why I never loved myself in the first place. Once I discovered the root, I was able to cultivate my own self-love.

How can you provide the feeling your ex gave you for yourself?

....

....

....

....

....

....

....

....

....

....

....

....

....

▶ *Turn to the Appendix for your next journal entry.*

PHASE 5
GIVE IT TO YOUR GOD

Do you believe there were any red flags that your intuition picked up before the relationship ended?

....

....

....

LIST THEM:

- ....

- ....

- ....

- ....

- ....

- ....

- ....

- ....

- ....

- ....

- ....

- ....

In the majority of unhealthy relationships, individuals see the red flags in the beginning. They ignore them because people have a tendency to justify the red flags in order to create the reality they want in their heads.

Don't worry, you're not alone. We have all ignored the reality of a person for the imaginary person we created them to be in our heads.

Why did you ignore the red flags in your relationship?

Why did you stay?

....

....

....

....

....

....

....

....

In terms of spirituality, I know everyone doesn't believe the same thing. I myself am a follower of Christ and I tend to pray about any and everything these days. Dating is a huge thing to pray about because it can be a life changing decision. I don't think people realize the impact being connected to the wrong person (or people) can have on your life. For this reason, I pray about men as soon as I meet them. Sometimes I don't even have to pray, my discernment will tell me yes or no.

So my question to you is simple, have you prayed or meditated for clarity on where you stand in your current scenario? If yes, what are you going to do with the answers you received? If you haven't prayed or meditated, why not?

....

....

....

....

....

....

....

....

In my last relationship, I actually prayed about him after week 1. God answered immediately with a big fat "NO!". Emphasis on the exclamation mark because God did not want me to have anything to do with my ex but I ignored it. After month 1, it was clear why God said no but I was already too attached. I was at a desperate point in my life where I wanted a relationship no matter what it took. In this instance, it took settling for the first guy who was interested in making me his girlfriend. I was so tired of just dating, just hanging out, and just having sex so I didn't care what God said, I was taking this relationship. It's not like there was anyone else who was willing to commit to me.

That ended up being the unhealthiest relationship I had ever experienced. I completely lost myself. That's what happens when you connect yourself with someone you're not compatible with. I learned a lot about myself, mainly what I don't want in a relationship. Too many people focus on what they want in a partner ignoring what type of rela-tionship they want. If you focus on the goal rather than the person, you're more likely to recognize if that person is fit for the puzzle you're creating. I was so focused on just getting a commitment that I didn't think about the quality of relationship I wanted. After that relationship, I realized it was everything I didn't want. I took the opposite of that and produced a list for the type of relationship I want in the future. Here are 5 things on my list...

1.   A relationship strong in communication

2.   A relationship where we hide nothing

3.   A relationship where we are friends at the foundation

4.   A relationship where we support one another in our careers

5.   A relationship where we both love God and pray together

If I meet someone who shuts down instead of communicates, I know they can't help me create the type of relationship I want so in the words of Ariana Grande, "Thank you, next!"

Now it's your turn, write out your list of what type of relation-ship you want.

- *A relationship* ....

....

- *A relationship* ....

....

- *A relationship* ....

....

- *A relationship* ....

....

- *A relationship* ....

....

- *A relationship* ....

....

-

Make sure you pray or meditate over your list so God can guide you on what to add or remove. Use this to measure compatibility with your future mates.

ASHLEIGH'S QUICK TIPS

Here are 5 things you can do spiritually to ease your mind when coping with a breakup:

1. Prayer

2. Listening to sermons on YouTube

3. Mindful Meditation

4. Journaling

5. Affirmations

▶ **Turn to the Appendix for your next journal entry.**

PHASE 6
PERCEPTION IS REALITY

TIP 1: THINK ABOUT THE BAD

Why was the relationship unhealthy?

....

....

What made you leave? If you didn't leave but they left,

why aren't you fighting to go back?

....

....

What things did they do that would make them a horrible forever spouse?

....

....

TIP 2: NOT EVERYONE YOU LOSE IS A LOSS...

The definition of *compatibility* is the ability of two things to be able to exist without problems or conflict. The definition of *love* is an intense feeling of deep affection. I don't know about you but I'm more interested in being in a relationship that checks off the compatibility box first before feeling any intense emotion. Society tells us that love is enough but is it? You can have deep affection for ice cream but that doesn't mean it can exist with your stomach without problem or conflict. Compatibility is necessary for a healthy relationship. That doesn't mean the relationship will be perfect, but it does mean it'll alleviate the majority of conflict and you guys will be harmonious in most occasions.

Were you and your ex compatible?

....

....

Now the next question requires introspection. My ex and I used to argue at least once a week. Do you know how draining that is?! So when we broke up, I lost weekly arguments. So your turn, think about what you lost.

What did you lose when the relationship ended?

....

....

What did you gain when the relationship ended?

....

....

TIP 3: THERE IS BETTER OUT THERE...

According to the US census of 2019, there are over 328.2 million people in the United States. That's just the United States, in the world there is reportedly 7.8 billion people. Out of all those people, you're going to sit here depressed over this one raggedy person who broke your heart? And ladies, I know society loves throwing that ratio in your face about more women than men but who cares?! All you need is 1. Just 1 person to be compatible with. There are more people out there to love your properly. Never lose hope.

TIP 4: REDISCOVER THE TRUE YOU...

In your last relationship, were you happy or were you comfortable?

....

....

....

Too many times we ignore our unhappiness because we are too comfortable to remove ourselves. One definition of comfortable is enjoying contentment and security. Many times we feel secure in an unhappy situation because it's predictable. The best example would be going to a job 5 days a week that you absolutely hate because it gives you a check every 2 weeks. Now you could leave and find a happier means of receiving an income but risks are scary. What if it takes longer than you expect to get another job? What if the new job requires more than you want to give? What if the new job is in another state? All of these can apply to leaving an unhappy and unhealthy but secure relationship, for an unpredictable but happier and healthier relationship.

It's always good to ask yourself that question in life, am I happy or comfortable?

HOW DO YOU REDISCOVER YOURSELF AFTER A BREAKUP?

I truly believe after every serious relationship, it shapes you into a new person. These changes aren't always extreme but there are changes to who you are after being with someone for a long period of time.

The best part of healing is discovering the new things about yourself now.

BELOW ARE QUESTIONS THAT CLARIFY WHO YOU ARE.

What are your favorite hobbies?

....

....

....

....

What are your favorite foods?

....

....

....

....

Who are your closest friends?

....

....

....

....

What are your career goals?

....

....

....

....

What are your goals for your physical, mental, and spiritual health?

....

....

....

....

What makes you happy?

....

....

....

....

TIP 5: YOU ARE WORTHY OF MORE...

Self-worth has become this watered down word that many people use but most have no idea what it means. Well I'm here to tell you about its importance. In a nutshell, self-worth is how you feel about who you are. When you think about what makes you (insert name here), how do you feel about it all? Do you like your body, your career, your flaws, your strengths, your relationship status, career, bank account, family history, etc.? In most scenarios, we don't actually sit down and ask ourselves "How do I feel about me today?" If we did, we'd avoid a lot of unnecessary entanglements.

As stated previously, when I dated my ex I didn't feel too good about myself. I was tired of just being used for sex and good conversation. I wanted to be someone's girlfriend so I accepted less. I wasn't aware that I was worthy of more because more wasn't being offered. We have to remember that even if less is being offered, that doesn't mean we have to accept it. It's our choice to raise our standards and be disciplined enough to wait for someone to meet them. I said all

of that to say, you're worthy of more than you required from
your ex. You may not see it now but you are.

LET'S EXPLORE THIS NOTION...

*What is something you said you'd never accept but you
accepted from this or another ex?*

....

....

....

....

*What is something you really want from a man but feel
too afraid to require or even ask for?*

....

....

....

How do you truly feel about yourself?

....

....

....

....

ASHLEIGH'S QUICK TIP

The only way to self-worth is understanding who you are as a person. You can only know yourself by spending intentional time with yourself. It is an excruciating process but necessary for growth. You deserve to know and love yourself more.

▶ **Turn to the Appendix for your next journal entry.**

PHASE 7
FIGHTING LONELY

Have you ever been driving on the interstate preparing to switch lanes after glancing at your side mirror? Then just as you're about to get over, a car suddenly passes you? You then think "that was a close one". You checked your review but you didn't look over your shoulder to check your blind spot. I hope this truly resonates because I am personally vexed daily by you none blind spot checkers. Look over your shoulder like your grandma Mable used to. Okay, back to the subject. Why am I talking about blind spots? Not only because you should seriously check it while driving but because there are also mental and emotional blind spots that many people are unaware of.

A blind spot is an area where a person's view is obstructed. Mentally and emotionally, it's a little harder to see because it's not actually visible, it's more of a reaction. The only way to really even detect your mental and emotional blind spots are to be intentional about how you respond to daily life events. Since blind spots come in different areas of life, today we'll focus solely on our lonely blind spots.

In the past, my biggest blind spots came in my lonely seasons. I had this pattern that I never noticed because my view was obstructed. I'd meet a guy, think he was great, we'd talk for a week or month, I'd find out he sucked after falling in lust with him, I'd be disappointed for a week and say "I'm going to be alone I just need me time", then I'd meet a guy a week later and the cycle would continue. I wasn't recognizing that my default reaction was to heal my brokenness with what broke me; a man.

Blind spots occur in vulnerable moments when you're allowing your emotions to control your decision making. In order to recognize blind spots, you have to sit still long enough and recognize patterns. Once you recognize an unhealthy pattern, then ask yourself discovery questions so you can eliminate the pattern.

What is your response to feeling lonely? (Remember, my previous response was to keep dating without healing although I saw that it wasn't working. Yours could be going back to an ex, partying a lot, drinking too much, etc…)

....

....

....

....

....

....

....

Do you feel like this is a healthy response? Why or Why not?

....

....

....

....

....

If you had to name something you want to stop doing in response to loneliness, what would it be?

....

....

....

....

....

When do you think you're most vulnerable after your breakups?

....

....

....

....

....

How can you use your knowledge of these vulnerable moments to help you recognize blind spots and eliminate unhealthy emotional response habits?

....

....

....

....

WHAT ARE YOU THINKING?

Ever heard of the phrase "think about what you're thinking about"? This is truly the best way to win at life. Contrary to popular belief, not every thought that goes through our mind is factual. On average, a person thinks 12,000 to 60,000 thoughts per day and I would bet that 30,000 of them are emotionally driven lies. How many times have you called yourself fat in your head for overeating when that's not true? How many times have you thought to yourself you'd never do something again because you were frustrated? How many times have you thought that no one loves you which you also know is a lie? Many of our thoughts lack logic and are emotionally fueled. Your job is to learn to recognize negative emotional thought patterns surrounding your breakup and reframing them to more logical thoughts.

Complete the chart below with thoughts surrounding your breakup. Reframe the emotional thoughts to more logical ones. I did the first one as an example.

Emotional Thoughts	Logical Thoughts
I'm going to die alone.	I feel lonely right now but I know it's only temporary.

▶ *Turn to the Appendix for your next journal entry.*

PHASE 8
SELF-REFLECTION

What lessons has this breakup taught you?

....

....

....

In most of my relationships or situationships, I wasn't the person who ruined it. I am not perfect by any means but I give a lot in all relationships so it's rare that I'm the culprit of losing a relationship. But you know what I have done wrong? Giving too much too soon, giving my affections to the wrong person, and projecting my love language unto others. Although these wouldn't normally be considered big mistakes in relationships, they are. These mistakes rob us of our own happiness. With this in mind, I'd like to ask you this very honest question.

What mistakes did you make in your last relationship?

....

....

....

....

How can you improve in future relationships after acknowledging these mistakes?

....

....

....

....

RECOGNIZING YOUR STRENGTHS

Too many times when we're going through scenarios that make us emotionally vulnerable, we tend to feel weak in all areas of life. This is not true at all. You are strong. You have overcome things far worse than this. This is the time to state your strengths.

NAME 5 SERIOUS AND/OR LIFE CHANGING EVENTS YOU'VE OVERCOME…

- *I have overcome* ....

  ....

- *I have overcome* ....

  ....

- *I have overcome* ....

  ....

- I have overcome ....

  ....

- I have overcome ....

  ....

What were your greatest strengths in your last relation-ship? (Even if you used these strengths on the wrong person)

....

....

....

....

....

....

....

AFFIRMATIONS

Affirmations may seem so cliché but they are necessary. Below, list 5 reasons you're strong inserting your name in the first blank.

- ....*is strong because* ....

....

- ....*is strong because* ....

....

- ....*is strong because* ....

....

- ....*is strong because* ....

....

- ....is strong because ....

  ....

- ....is strong because ....

  ....

- ....is strong because ....

  ....

- ....is strong because ....

  ....

▶ ***Turn to the Appendix for your next journal entry.***

PHASE 9
SIT IN IT

Do you stretch after working out? If you do, I'm proud of you. When I'm in the gym, 80% of people walk out right after a rigorous workout. Stretching is inconvenient as well as painful. But you'll thank yourself the next day when you're able to walk straight. When you have an intense workout, your body produces lactic acid. This is what causes the pain you feel later in the day and on the next day. Stretching after the workout, although inconvenient and painful, eliminates lactic acid and reduces the pain.

After a heartbreak, sitting in the pain may seem inconvenient and painful in the moment but the long term benefits make it worth it. I'm sure most people don't automatically think

"I'm sad, let me sit here and sulk." We're conditioned to avoid pain and chase feelings of happiness. As stated in *Phase 9*, it's okay to *not* be okay and sitting in the pain is a necessity.

What's your default response to emotional pain?

....

....

....

....

....

....

....

....

I think the best way to change a habit is to be prepared when it comes up. A great way to do that is to create an action plan. We'll call this the emotional response action plan.

EMOTIONAL RESPONSE ACTION PLAN

I've filled out the first 2 columns. Feel free to repeat the objectives and emotions but with your own default response and new response.

OBJECTIVES	EMOTION	DEFAULT RESPONSE	NEW RESPONSE
Get over my ex completely	Sadness	Drink Wine	Go for a walk
Heal fully so I won't make the same mistakes	Anger	Send ex an angry text	Write frustrations in a journal

A LESSON ON PACING

I've always been a hopeless romantic and I hated it for a long time. When I was younger, it kept me innocent and hopeful. As I grew older and started dating, it kept me picking the wrong men and giving too much benefit of the doubt. I had a bad habit of romanticizing people and relationships due to my heavy pursuit of a romantic partner. It caused me to give too much too soon and trust too quickly. Sadly, not everyone has great intentions so we have to guard our hearts as to not fall into romanticizing traps. The best way to do that is by pacing yourself.

In a recent therapy session, my therapist told me that I need to examine my level of trust and compare it to my level of emotional investment. For example, if I wouldn't trust this person to drive my car, why are we discussing being exclusive with one another. Intimacy levels and trust should match. I can admit that I've allowed my yearning for affection and companionship to outweigh my need to evaluate a man and how much I can actually trust if what he's saying is true. So let's use this knowledge to set the tone for how you'll pace yourself in your future relationships to avoid falling for the wrong person.

FILL IN THE BLANKS FOR THE FOLLOWING:

I understand everyone has different values and goals for where they want their relationships to go. But if the goal is a healthy and happy relationship with a lower probability of heartbreak, then you have to make some changes. One controllable change you can make is how you evaluate who you will commit to next.

I've filled out the first two, you try it now.

If .... *we haven't established where this relationship is going* then we shouldn't ...... *be having sex*

If .... *I haven't been around him long enough to understand his values and evaluate his character* then we shouldn't ...... *we shouldn't be introducing one another to friends and family*

If ....

....

then we shouldn't ....

....

If ....

....

then we shouldn't ....

....

If ....

....

then we shouldn't ....

....

THE DISCIPLINE MUSCLE

Discipline is a muscle. You have to continuously build it. On every level of growth, it becomes harder. But in order to start building it, you have to start with small parts of your life. A few examples are things like time management, exercise, committing to reading more, etc. If you want to discipline yourself enough to not go back to your ex or to avoid settling, you have to have practice in other areas. Let's make a list of things you can start applying discipline to today.

Just a tip, start with something simple and doable. If you know you hate dieting, don't start there. Start with something small and work your way up. When lifting weights, beginners start with 5 pounds, not 50.

- I will commit to being discipline in ...*going to bed by 11pm*..

- *I will commit to being discipline in* ....

....

- *I will commit to being discipline in* ....

....

- *I will commit to being discipline in* ....

....

- *I will commit to being discipline in* ....

....

- *I will commit to being discipline in* ....

....

▶ **Turn to the Appendix for your next journal entry.**

PHASE 10
RECLAIM YOUR THOUGHTS

We spoke about mindfulness but I want to repeat its importance. Everything we do and feel flows from our thoughts. In order to get your mind back to a healthy and happy place, you have to master the art of recognizing negative thought patterns. That is the only way to release the ones that are detrimental. This will not only help in your love life, but in all parts of your life.

For this to work, I want you to commit to your growth by signing this meditation contract. It's a commitment to yourself; a commitment to mental and emotional growth.

I, ______________________________

will commit to doing a mindfulness meditation at least 5

times a week for one month.

Sign Your Name Here:

____

As stated in *Phase 10*, there are several free guided medita-

tions on YouTube. But you can do the example below each

time if you'd like. Just gradually increase your time.

MINDFULNESS EXERCISE: LETTING GO

This exercise was adapted from *Mindful Coaching: How Mindfulness Can Transform Coaching Practice* by Liz Hall

Let's try letting go for a few minutes.

Choose a comfortable place to sit upright. Gently close your eyes and loosen your muscles. Take three deep breaths. Scan your body for tense areas you may feel and release them once you notice. Calmly pay attention to each breath and as you exhale, say to yourself "letting go of (insert ex name)". Do this a few more times and notice how you feel. Once you're ready, come out of this meditation gently and record what you've noticed.

MINDFULNESS CALENDAR

Mindfulness	Mindfulness	Mindfulness	Mindfulness	Mindfulness
☐ 1 min ☐ 3 mins ☐ 5 mins	☐ 1 min ☐ 3 mins ☐ 5 mins	☐ 1 min ☐ 3 mins ☐ 5 mins	☐ 1 min ☐ 3 mins ☐ 5 mins	☐ 1 min ☐ 3 mins ☐ 5 mins
Mindfulness	Mindfulness	Mindfulness	Mindfulness	Mindfulness
☐ 1 min ☐ 3 mins ☐ 5 mins	☐ 1 min ☐ 3 mins ☐ 5 mins	☐ 1 min ☐ 3 mins ☐ 5 mins	☐ 1 min ☐ 3 mins ☐ 5 mins	☐ 1 min ☐ 3 mins ☐ 5 mins
Mindfulness	Mindfulness	Mindfulness	Mindfulness	Mindfulness
☐ 1 min ☐ 3 mins ☐ 5 mins	☐ 1 min ☐ 3 mins ☐ 5 mins	☐ 1 min ☐ 3 mins ☐ 5 mins	☐ 1 min ☐ 3 mins ☐ 5 mins	☐ 1 min ☐ 3 mins ☐ 5 mins
Mindfulness	Mindfulness	Mindfulness	Mindfulness	Mindfulness
☐ 1 min ☐ 3 mins ☐ 5 mins	☐ 1 min ☐ 3 mins ☐ 5 mins	☐ 1 min ☐ 3 mins ☐ 5 mins	☐ 1 min ☐ 3 mins ☐ 5 mins	☐ 1 min ☐ 3 mins ☐ 5 mins

What harmful thoughts are you noticing?

- ....

....

- ....

....

- ....

....

- ....

....

- ....

....

▶ ***Turn to the Appendix for your next journal entry.***

CONCLUSION

You've read the book and completed the workbook assign-ments. Now it's time to apply what you've learned. Write your final journal entry here by answering the following questions.

How will you apply what you've learned in this process?

....

....

....

....

....

....

....

....

....

After all of your reflection, why are you x'ing your ex?

- ....

....

- ....

....

- ....

....

- ....

....

- ....

....

- ....

....

- ....

How will you emerge as a better (insert your name here) after you've healed completely from this relationship?

- ....

....

- ....

....

- ....

....

- ....

....

- ....

....

Go back to those thoughts and draw a line through them. They are no longer serving you and you are letting them go.

APPENDIX

Journal Entry 1: Intro

How do you feel? No really, how do you actually feel?

Pour it all out in this week's journal entry.

....
....
....
....
....
....
....
....
....
....
....
....
....
....
....
....
....

Journal Entry 2: Let it Out

What is the main thing you wish you could convey to your ex that you don't feel they comprehend?

Take some time and think about what life will look like being single. In a perfect world where being single was the goal, what would that look like? What would you be accomplishing? How would you feel knowing you are in full control of your peace and happiness?

....

....

....

....

....

....

....

....

....

....

....

....

Journal Entry 4: Rebounds are Only Good in Basketball

Have you ever gone cold turkey and stopped dating? I mean a full shutdown on your love life. No texting anyone you're romantically interested in, no communicating with exes, no giving your number out, no flirting, no dating apps; NOTHING. If you have, what was that experience like and what did it teach you? If you have not, why haven't you taken a dating break and would you consider it?

....

....

....

....

....

....

....

....

....

....

Journal Entry 5: The Closure Trap

If your ex passed away 1 minute after your breakup and there was no way possible for you to get "closure" from them directly, how would you go about healing from the relationship?

Journal Entry 6: Give it to Your God

What emotions or struggles do you feel stuck dealing with that won't go away? Write them out as if you're talking to God and asking Him to help you cope with them.

Journal Entry 7: Perception is Reality

What was your perception of your previous relationship while you were in it? What is your perception now?

Journal Entry 8: Fighting Lonely

I've been single for 90% of my adult life. If anyone knows that it's tough being by yourself, it's me. It is okay to have down days but the goal is to not remain there. What is the hardest part of being alone? Reflect on the emotions you feel when you think of the times when you are by yourself.

Journal Entry 9: Self-Reflection

"I wish I knew then, what I know now."

This is the popular saying most of us repeat after being on the other side of a life event that we regret or that changed us. I know I say this after break ups. I always wish I had a time machine so I could redo the relationship or just completely avoid the relationship. Since I don't possess a time machine to help you go back in time, I'm just going to ask you to speak to your old self. Knowing what you know now, what would you say to the you in the relationship? How would you encourage that you? Would you tell yourself to leave sooner or keep fighting? Would you suggest more self-love or more boundaries? Speak to the past you from your current perspective being outside of the relationship.

Journal Entry 10: Sit in It

What is something that you've noticed after sitting in the pain that you wouldn't have recognized if you were too busy trying to be happy again?

Journal Entry 11: Reclaim Your Thoughts

One of the most aggravating things about a breakup is all the plans you had with your ex. All the places you planned to go or activities you wanted to try with him or her. All is not lost. Who says you can't do it without them?

Create a 90 Day bucket list of things you plan to do with your friends or on your own.

AFTER BREAKUP BUCKET LIST

- ....

....

- ....

....

- ....

....

- ....
....

- ....
....

- ....
....

- ....
....

- ....
....

- ....
....

- ....
....

- ....

....

- ....

....

- ....

....

- ....

....

- ....

....

- ....

....

- ....

....

.

- •	....

....

- •	....

....

- •	....

....

- •	....

....

- •	....

....

- •	....

....

- •	....

....

9 798561 797088